Pearl and Beadstringing
with Henrietta

by Henrietta Virchick

Pearl and Beadstringing with Henrietta

by Henrietta Virchick

Graphic Illustrations by:

Gail Kaufer

Photography by:

Tim Long Photography

Contributing Designers:

Judy Brownlie
Janice DiGiovanni
Birdee Krause
Jo Russo

Printed in the U.S.A.

CONTENTS

Introduction

My romance with precious and semi-precious beads started many years ago while working for a leading wholesale diamond importer at Rockefeller Center in New York City just a few blocks away from 47th Street, one of the most famous diamond and jewelry streets in the world. It was here that I served my "apprenticeship" in the diamond and jewelry business picking up bits of information from talented craftsmen and designers. I became the "jeweler" and "shopper" for my family and friends asking knowledgeable people around me "where" and "how to", learning the tricks of the trade, and loving the challenge.

My first encounter with beads and their design came when I had the opportunity to buy two strands of unstrung, gem quality lapis lazuli beads at a good price. Falling in love with their magnificent royal blue color flecked with gold, I set off for 47th Street to a jewelry findings house to purchase some 14 Kt gold beads to intersperse with the lapis and a special 14 Kt gold clasp. I took my purchases to a pearl and bead stringer, one of the many who sit in their little booths in the different jewelry exchanges plying their trade. She suggested I work out the design myself and temporarily string the beads on a piece of thread to save her time and me money.

That evening as I laid out the beads, arranging and rearranging them, I suddenly remembered a little bag of cultured pearls left over from the original stringing of my pearls and found there were just enough to make a beautiful pattern of lapis, gold and pearls. When I saw the finished necklace, I was thrilled by its beauty and very proud of my design. (To this day I never fail to receive a compliment each time I wear it.) From then on, I was addicted to beads. You just can't stop with one necklace. I used to wander in and out of the exchanges to the different bead dealers looking at all the beautiful beads hanging up, studying their quality, asking where they came from and comparing prices. Most of the dealers got to know me and sometimes I think they gave me prices I couldn't resist just to get rid of me. The only thing that bothered me was having to pay the price of stringing the beads. Sometimes the cost of stringing was more than the cost of the stone beads plus the 14 Kt gold beads combined, but even so, I still spent only a fraction of the necklace's retail value!

Eventually I did learn the art of stringing and it made my hobby that much more rewarding and affordable, enabling me to change the length or design at a whim.

Years later when I retired, I decided it would be fun to teach the craft and share the joys of beading with others. I brought all the beautiful necklaces I had designed and strung to the director of the Community Services Program at Brookdale Community College in Lincroft, New Jersey, near my home. She was impressed that anyone could learn to do this and suggested I write a program. This program evolved into a very successful craft series, and each time the course was offered it was booked solid in a matter of days. Many students came to class with broken necklaces and bracelets they had taken to a jewelry store for repair, but had decided against having the work done because it was too expensive. Some told me they had gone to the library in search of a book that might teach them how to restring their beads, but were unable to find any. The only place you could take such a course was in jewelry schools, many charging hundreds of dollars just for the pearl and bead stringing course alone.

While teaching, I realized what a tremendous interest there was in this craft and how easy it was to learn when it was taught visually. Thinking of the many people who could learn right in their own homes with a videocassette, I made a video called "*Pearl and Bead Stringing with Henrietta*". This 50 minute VHS tape is available at bead supply dealers and hobby and craft shops around the country.

At the urging of many of my students who wanted a permanent record of what they had learned and from so many wonderful letters from subscribers of the video asking for more information, I set forth here to give all of them, and you, a most graphic and professional description of pearl and bead stringing, along with many helpful hints and ideas for your personal and professional use.

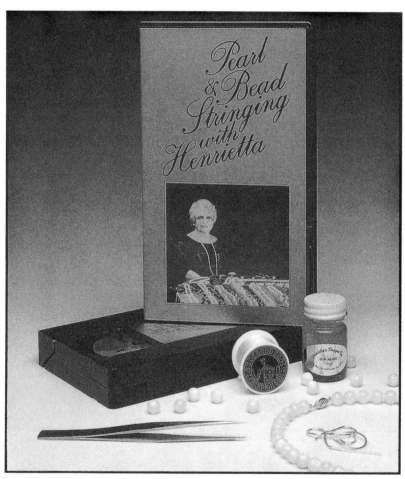

"Pearl and Bead Stringing with Henrietta"

Chapter 1: Guidelines For Professional Custom Pearl and Beadstringing

Welcome to the wonderful and exciting world of beads! There are so many beautiful stone beads to choose from. They come in an array of exciting colors, shapes and sizes to please the simplest or the most avant-garde tastes and their sources will be made known to you. An assortment of several kinds of bead necklaces is very affordable when you make your own. You have the advantage of being able to design, redesign, lengthen or shorten them in a matter of a hour or so as your wardrobe dictates.

As a teacher and designer, I delight in seeing my students' imaginative creations, never ceasing to be amazed at the endless combinations of precious and semi-precious beads that result in their own exquisitely unique designs. I love hearing of their entrepreneurial success, which you too can achieve when I show you how easy it is to get started.

You will be taken through each project with explicit graphics, making it easy to string along, step by step. In some instances, you will be taught more than one method, and if you learn them all you may even develop a style of your own, using a combination of these methods. It's simply a matter of choice, but if you want your work to be professional, there are a few guidelines to follow:

1. All precious and semi-precious beads, including stone beads interspersed with some gold or silver beads, should be strung on silk thread. It is the strongest; it knots the best; and the finished beads hang the smoothest. Though nylon thread is cheaper, it is unacceptable as it attracts more dust, dirt and body oil which are harmful to pearls and more porous beads such as turquoise and coral. Though many stringers do use nylon thread, it is only second best.

2. When a clasp is used, it should always be attached with French wire. There is no substitute for silk thread and French wire in custom beading and it's easy to learn to use, making your work a cut above others.

When this is pointed out to your customer, it gives a standard by which to measure the quality and professionalism of your work.

3. When using precious beads such as silver or gold or any other metal beads, they should be strung on chain, foxtail preferably, because it stretches the least. The chain should be soldered to the jump rings of the clasp, or if no clasp is used, the two ends should be soldered together leaving enough extra chain to make the beads flexible in either case.

4. Very heavy beads should be strung on nylon coated jewelry wire (tiger tail) or soft monofilament and the clasp attached with bead tips. The bead tip I prefer is the clam type. The knot is placed in the clam and then squeezed shut with a chain nose plier, forming a little bead, concealing the knot entirely. The bead tip is then attached to the clasp. Bead tips are never used professionally on silk thread.

You will learn to do all this and much more for your personal or professional use. Most of all, you are in for some unexpected pleasures and a whole lot of fun, so let's get started!

Chapter 2: Tools Of The Trade

You can make high-fashion, precious and semi-precious necklaces exactly like professionals do for a fraction of their retail cost or you can simply learn to restring your own pearls and beads for tremendous savings. Though it only takes a minimum of tools to learn pearl and bead stringing, as you become proficient in the art, you will want to own many others. They are all relatively inexpensive, easy to use and some will help to expand your skills to make coordinating bracelets and earrings to wear, give as a gift or sell for fun and profit!

Here are some of the tools and materials used or mentioned in this book which will enable you to string along with me step-by-step.

Beading Board - It is used to hold beads, lay out designs and make your work portable. Styles in wood, wood covered in velvet and plastic are available.

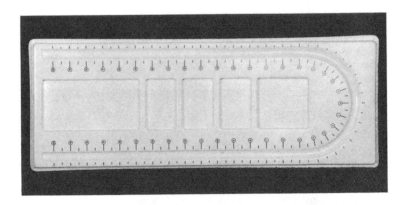

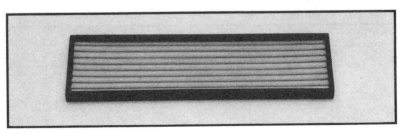

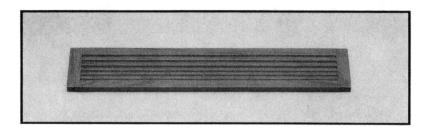

Jeweler's Stainless Steel Beading Tweezers Size AA - Used to make knots between beads.

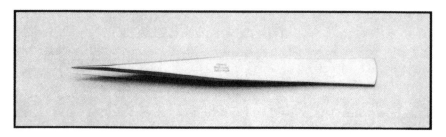

Awl - Knot Tamper - Made of stainless steel, used to apply glue, tamp in knot ends and to make knots.

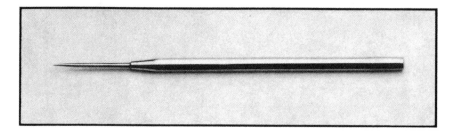

Bead Pick Up Tweezers - Stainless steel tool to pick up beads. It is helpful in arranging designs on a bead board.

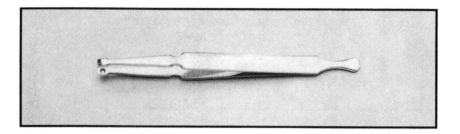

Beading Needles - Stainless steel needles available in sizes: fine #6, medium fine #8, medium #10 and large #12. Available in brass also.

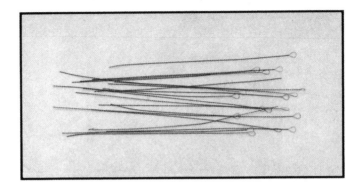

French Wire - A fine wire coiled into a flexible hollow tube in gold or silver color used to hide and strengthen the thread around clasp rings.

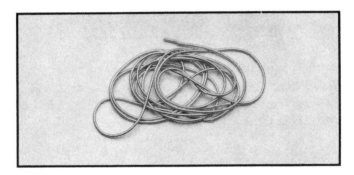

Millimeter Gauge - Used to measure size of beads, especially graduated pearls.

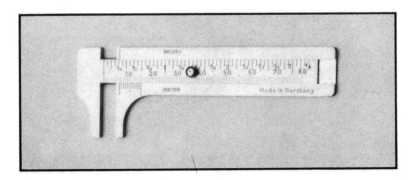

Gum Arabic - This new glue product was developed by Henrietta's Designs Inc. specifically for fine bead-stringing on silk thread. It is used to make self thread needles, and makes closing knot ends invisible. Washes off hands, tools and beads easily.

Chain Nose Pliers - Used to open jump rings, to attach bead tips to clasps, to make earrings and other jewelry. Helpful to pull thread through beads at times.

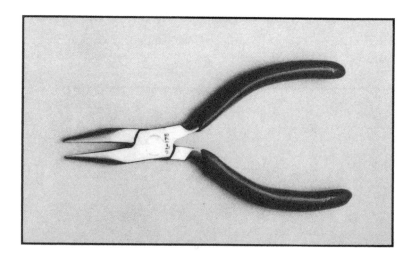

Round Nose Pliers - Used to attach some bead tips to clasps and to make earrings and other jewelry.

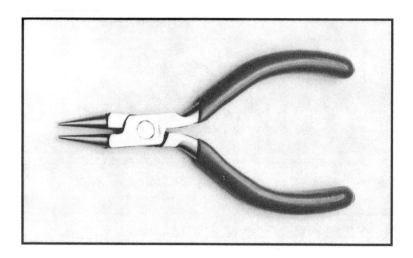

Side Cutting Diagonal Wire Nippers - For cutting jewelry wire and head pins.

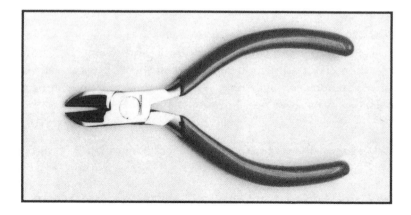

Bead Tips - Used to attach jewelry wire to clasps. Available in cup and clam type in yellow or gold colored metal. May be found in 14 Kt gold.

Crystal Cement - *(G-S Hypo-Tube Cement)* - Used as a glue on jewelry wire and fuses knots on monofilament.

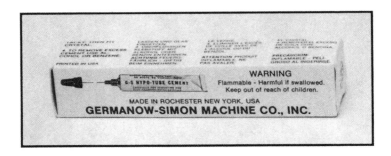

Clasps - They come in a multitude of shapes and sizes for single or multiple strands from the most common spring ring type to more elaborate and decorative ones worn as an accent piece to the side or front of the necklace in 14 Kt gold, Sterling silver and non-precious metals.

Bead Crimps - Used to attach more rigid monofilaments to clasps.

Head Pins - Used to string beads on that are attached to earrings, in 2.5" to 3.0" lengths of 14 Kt gold and gold filled, sterling silver and other metals.

Earring Components - Various style earrings that beads can be attached to or from.

Straight Edged Sharp Kitchen Paring Knife - Used to sharpen silk thread to make a self needle.

Ruler or Yardstick - For measuring thread; necklaces; and bracelets.

Sharp Curved Manicuring Scissors - Best for cutting threads close to knots.

STRINGING MATERIALS

The leading name in every type of bead stringing material is Gudebrod, Inc., an esteemed old firm established in 1870 and handed down from generation to generation. They are noted for their famous Champion silk thread which is used to string the finest gemstone beads of the world. Recently they developed a revolutionary new stringing material which deserves special mention, a woven nylon filament called "*C-Thru-B Translucent Cord*" that has the strength of tiger tail and monofilament with much less stretch. Its uniqueness lies in the fact that it can be knotted, allowing the necklace to hang with a suppleness as if it were strung on silk thread.

Spool Champion Silk Bead Cord - Black/White/Colors in various sizes for custom gemstone bead stringing.

Spool Champion Nylon Bead Cord - Black/White/Colors in various sizes for inexpensive bead stringing.

Carded Champion Silk Bead Cord - Black/White/Colors in various sizes, 5 yd single strand for the non-professional wishing to custom string an individual strand of beads professionally and economically. A new product many will be happy to learn about.

Carded Silk or Nylon Bead Cord with Brass Beading Needle Attached - Black/White/Colors in various sizes. A double strand twisted into a single 72" length. Used best for stringing beads requiring no knotting.

C-Thru-B Translucent Cord - Comes in extra fine, fine, medium and large sizes. Used to string heavier beads, weaving beads and it can be knotted between the beads. Can be attached to clasp without bead tips or crimps.

Tiger Tail - Nylon coated jewelry wire available in 12, 18, 27, and 40 lb. test used to string bracelets and heavy beads.

Gem Monofilament - Size 6, 25 yds. per spool. Used to weave beads.

See inside back cover for Gudebrod's Color Charts

Chapter 3: Learning The Art of Hand Knotting

1. How To Measure The Thread

2. How To Make A Thread Needle

3. How To Make The Knots Using A Tweezer One Bead At A Time

4. How To Cut Your Work Apart

5. How To Make The Knots Using An Awl One Bead At A Time

6. How To Make The Knots Using Your Fingers One Bead At A Time

7. How To String All The Beads On The Thread Before Knotting.

Materials:

Yardstick or Ruler

Gudebrod's Champion White Silk Thread Size FF

Sharp Curved Manicuring Scissors

Square of Formica, Pocket Mirror or Piece of Glass

Straight Edged Kitchen Paring Knife

Beading Awl (Knot Tamper)

Gum Arabic Glue

Beading Board or Small Hand Towel
(To Keep Beads From Rolling)

16" Strand of 8MM Mother of Pearl Beads

Size AA Stainless Steel Jewelers Beading Tweezer

Wiping Cloth or Napkin

Suggestion: To keep the work from slipping, work on a table-
cloth, under a good light, such as a fluorescent or
halogen desk lamp.

To practice knotting we need beads with uniform drill holes, a
millimeter size easy to handle and heavier thread enabling you to see
just how good your knots are. Therefore, I have chosen 8MM Mother
of Pearl beads which take size FF white thread for you to learn with.
If you select another kind of bead, check the drill holes and use the
proper size thread. Your bead supplier should be able to guide you
in the beginning.

1. HOW TO MEASURE THE THREAD

Beads should always be strung on a double strand of silk
thread. If you line the unstrung beads up on your beadboard you can
measure them. 16" of unstrung beads will require 79" of thread. The
rule of thumb to determine the amount of thread needed is to
multiply the length of the unstrung beads, in this case 16", by four and
add 15", or 4 x 16" + 15" = 79".

2. HOW TO MAKE A THREAD NEEDLE

Fig. 1a. Bring the two ends of the thread together on a smooth surface. I use a square of formica which is a counter top color sample I purchased in a kitchen design store for 25 cents.

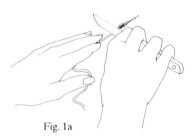

Fig. 1a

You may use a pocket mirror, piece of glass, or any other smooth surface. Start to shave approximately 1 1/2" of the thread by gently gliding the paring knife over the thread until the nubs have been removed from the silk and the thread has been thinned. If your knife is very sharp press lightly, if dull a little harder. The more you shave the thinner your needle will be. With your knot tamper (awl) dab a small drop of gum arabic on the ends, wipe your fingers free of any excess glue on a cloth and twist the threads to make a needle, cutting off any stray wisps. If you apply too much glue your needle will be too thick. Let dry for a few minutes until stiff. Later on you will be taught how to use a wire beading needle, and if you choose to do your beading with one, it is still very important that you learn to make a thread needle as sometimes the eye of the wire needle breaks and comes off the thread. It is impossible to attach a new wire needle in the middle of your work, so you must make a thread needle to continue, or cut you work apart and start all over again. I prefer making my own thread needle to using a wire one as I never run out of needles and don't have to cope with bent, twisted and broken wire needles. You will also find it makes beading so much simpler.

3. HOW TO MAKE THE KNOTS USING A TWEEZER ONE BEAD AT A TIME

Fig. 1. Holding the two threads from the needle even, tie them together in a simple overhand knot close to the bottom and string the first bead on. Hold your left hand in front of your face and lay the needle over the palm of your hand.

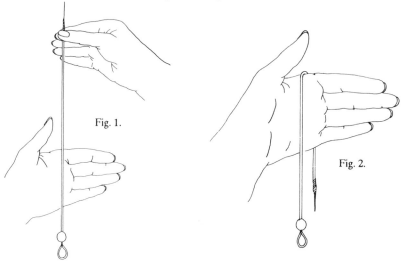

Fig. 1.

Fig. 2.

Fig. 2. Bring the needle down the back of your hand.

Fig. 3. Bring the needle back up the front of your hand and place it under the thread on the palm of your hand, from left to right.

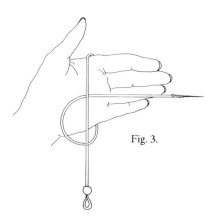

Fig. 3.

Fig. 4. Pull the needle and thread to the right to make a large loop around your hand, then drop the needle to the **left** side of your body.

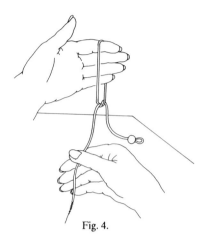

Fig. 4.

Fig 5.   Place your right hand through the back of the loop, removing the loop from the left hand onto the right hand. It should look like a circle with two threads coming out of the front and two threads coming out of the back.

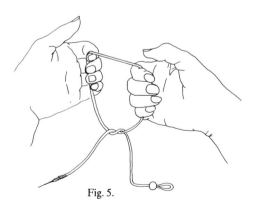

Fig. 5.

Fig. 6. Resting the side of your right hand on the first bead to keep it from slipping, grasp the threads close to the loop with the first three fingers of your left hand and pull the thread taut. By spreading the fingers of your right hand within the loop and then moving them back together while pulling the thread in your left hand, you can adjust the size of the loop and even the threads coming out of the bead. It is important that the two threads coming out of the bead be the same length to make a good knot. As more beads are added on, the strand will become heavier and it will not be necessary to hold them with the side of your hand.

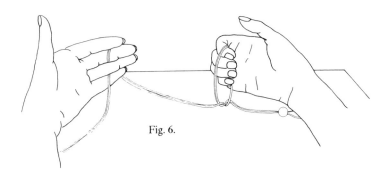

Fig. 6.

Fig. 7. Still holding the thread between your left three fingers, lay the loop from your right hand over the work (the one bead strung), and use the index finger of your left hand to spread the circle (loop). ("over the work" refers to the bead or beads already strung). In other words, the loop should be on top of the work as in Fig. 7, not as in Fig. 7a in back of the work, or as in 7b in front of the work. With index finger and thumb of left hand grasp the threads coming out of the bead within the circle. Pick the tweezer up with your right hand. Put the tweezer points in the circle and grasp the threads coming out of the bead with it, pushing it back up against the bead to the right, while pulling the thread with your thumb and index finger to the left. Tweezer should be raised slightly off the table. Do not dig tweezer into the table as you will damage the tips of the tweezer.

Fig. 7.

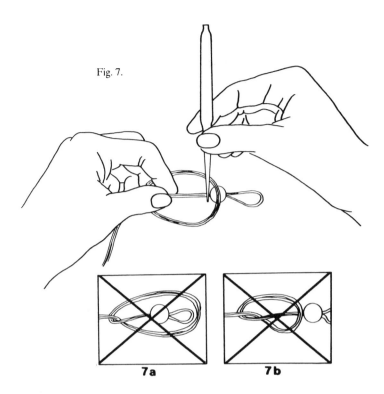

7a   **7b**

Fig. 8. Still holding the thread with the left three fingers and with the tweezer in position, simply remove the thumb and index finger from the circle and pull the thread to the left to close the circle (loop) around the tips of the tweezer. If you should let go of the threads in your left hand, the threads around the tweezer tips may not be even. You would then have to pull each thread individually to make sure they are even before removing the tweezer.

Fig. 8.

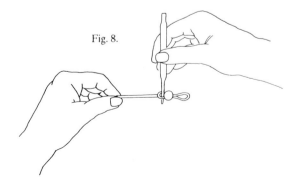

Fig. 9. Bring your left thumbnail in front of the loop around the tweezer and as you pull the tweezer up with you right hand to remove it from the loop push the knot towards the hole of the bead with your left thumbnail simultaneously, pushing in as you pull up.

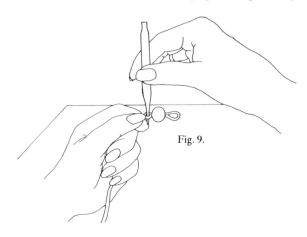

Fig. 9.

Fig. 10. Immediately open the two threads and pull them apart with just enough pressure to tighten the knot. Don't stop to examine the knot before pulling apart as you may pull the knot away from the bead. Some beaders do not open the threads to tighten the knot but simply put the next bead on pushing it tight up against the last bead strung, pulling the bead to the right while pulling the needle thread to the left. Other beaders place the tweezer in front of the knot, pushing the knot to the right while pulling the needle thread to the left. I have tested both these methods and have found them unsatisfactory because not enough slack in the knot is removed, and too soon the space between the knot and the bead becomes too great, making it seem as though the thread has stretched when in reality only the knot has tightened from the weight of the beads. Eventually with wear, the thread does stretch, so why hurry it along by improperly tightening the knot? The only reason you would tighten the knot with a bead or tweezer is if you were using a single strand of thread, leaving you no alternative. Continue to string and knot until all the beads are strung.

Using the tweezer to knot is probably the most popular method, the first choice of many beaders.

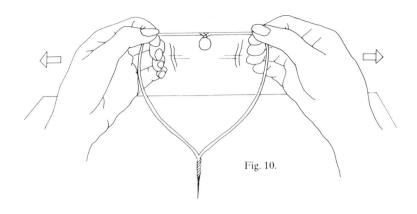

Fig. 10.

4. HOW TO CUT YOUR WORK APART

If you are satisfied with you work you can move on to practice using an awl to make the knots. In any event, you must cut your work apart, and there is a right and wrong way to do this.

Place the scissors between the bead and the knot and cut. In other words in back of the knot and in front of the bead. You will then have a tail to hold while cutting off the next bead. On a finished neclace, with no clasp, cut directly through the center of the knot between two beads to get started. If you place your scissors in front of the knot and cut, the knot will go into the bead hole and get stuck and no amount of pushing with a needle or pin will push the knot out of the hole. If this happens to a very expensive bead or pearl don't panic. Bring the bead to your jeweler or a jewelry repair shop and in a matter of seconds they will drill the knot out, with no harm to the bead. This has happened to me a few times and though my jeweler would not charge me, I asked how much I could tell my students it would cost. He shrugged his shoulders and laughingly said "three for a dollar". So if there is no crisis, save up three before you take them to be drilled!

5. HOW TO MAKE THE KNOTS USING AN AWL ONE BEAD AT A TIME

Fig. 11. Go back to Fig. 1a and proceed through Fig. 4, placing the awl in the circle with your right hand while removing your left hand and slide the loop with the awl to the right tightly up to the bead while pulling the needle thread tightly to the left with your left hand.

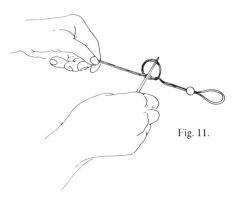

Fig. 11.

Fig. 12. Push the knot into the hole of the bead with your left thumbnail while removing the awl by pulling it toward you. Open the threads to tighten the knot as in Fig. 10.

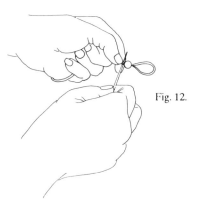

Fig. 12.

Though this may seem easier than using the tweezer and some beaders do use an awl, most prefer using the tweezer as it makes a tighter and better knot, but you may decide for yourself.

6. HOW TO MAKE THE KNOTS USING YOUR FINGERS ONE BEAD AT A TIME

Fig. 13. Go back to Fig. 1a and proceed through Fig. 3 continuing to pull the needle thread to the right, closing the four fingers of your left hand around the thread on the palm of your hand. If the needle thread is too long, drop the thread and pick it up again closer to the thread on your hand.

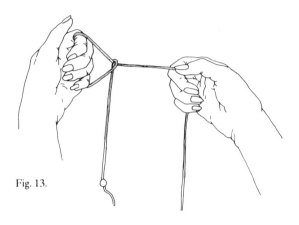

Fig. 13.

Fig. 14. By pulling the needle thread to the right and turning the left hand down slightly, we bring the knot tight up against the bead hole. By opening and closing the fingers of your left hand in the circle and pulling the needle thread up and down with your right hand we can adjust the size of the circle (loop) to allow room for fingers to slip out.

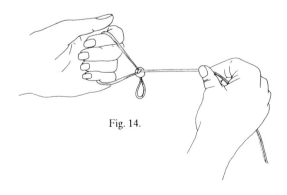

Fig. 14.

Fig. 15. Slip the index and forefinger of the left hand out of the circle.

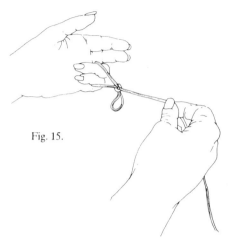

Fig. 15.

Fig. 16. Bring the index finger and forefinger around the bead to hold it, and with the remaining two fingers still in the circle, pull the circle taut by pulling the two fingers to the left while pulling the needle thread to the right. Make sure the knot is tight and directly over the bead hole and the circle is large enough to allow the last two fingers to exit. You can use the front of your left thumb to spread the thread at the bead hole to bring the knot tight up against the hole and to push the bead up close to the last bead strung, or in this case up to the knot.

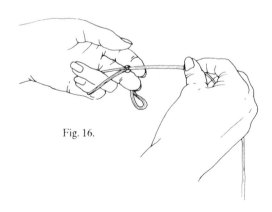

Fig. 16.

Fig. 17. Place the thumb of your left hand directly on top of the knot at the bead hole, pressing down to hold the knot in place.

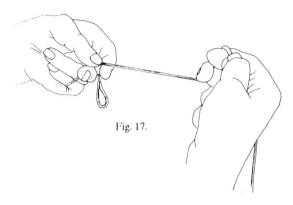

Fig. 17.

Fig. 18. Drop the last two fingers of your left hand out of the circle and pull the needle thread to the right as hard as you can, (not too fast or the bead may slip), to form the knot close to the bead hole.

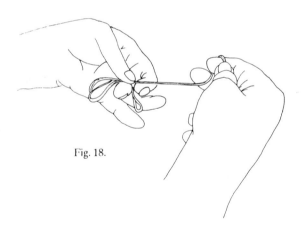

Fig. 18.

Even though some beaders suggest no further tightening is necessary and I have become very adept using this method, I still prefer to open the threads to tighten the knot as in Fig. 10 and occasionally I do feel the knot tightening. Remember, we are learning custom beading and the emphasis is on quality rather than speed.

7. HOW TO STRING ALL THE BEADS ON THE THREAD BEFORE KNOTTING

Fig. 19. Work through Fig. 1, but continue to string all the beads on the silk before knotting. After stringing the last bead, make a slip knot near the needle end to keep the beads from falling off. Push all but the first bead back towards the slip knot.

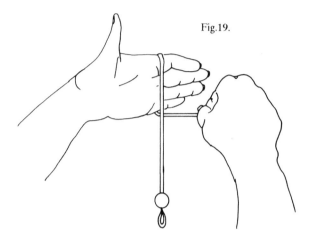

Fig.19.

Holding your left palm in front of your face, lay the thread with the first bead strung over the palm of your hand, bring it down the back of your hand and turn your left hand away from your face to the left to form a figure 4 with the thread.

Fig. 20. Hold the two threads that crossover together between your right thumb and index finger.

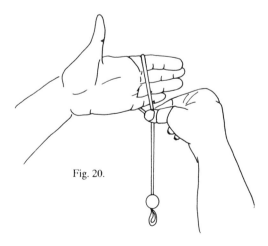

Fig. 20.

Fig. 21. Reach your left thumb into the top part of the 4 (loop) and place it in front of the bead and thread hanging down. Flip the thread and bead back, rolling it over your thumb to bring it through and out of the loop. Continue on to finger knot, or by dropping the needle to the left side of your body and laying the loop over the work, to knot with tweezer or awl, opening the threads to tighten the knot. Bring the next bead down and repeat the procedure.

Remember to keep your two threads even at all times or you will end up with a loop next to the knot and bead hole.

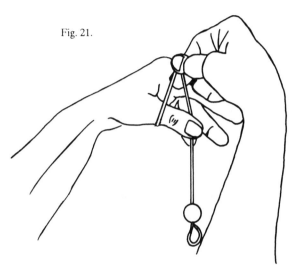

Fig. 21.

When making a very long necklace and more than half of the beads have been knotted you may find it easier to start to bring the shorter end of the unknotted beads through the 4 (loop) in this manner: make the figure 4 with your left hand as we did before but hold the thread that crosses over together with the thumb and forefinger of the same hand (left). Bring the needle and the unknotted beads through the front of the loop and continue knotting in the same fashion you were before.

This is unquestionably the fastest way to knot, as there is no tool to pick up or put down, but it also takes the most practice. However, you can do this in your favorite chair while watching television.

Finger knotting is a mystery to many experienced beaders, but not to you!

Chapter 4: Learning To Attach A Clasp With French Wire Using A Thread Needle

Materials:

16" 8MM Mother of Pearl Beads

79" Gudebrod's Champion White Silk Thread Size FF

1 Gold Fishhook Clasp

Medium Size Gold French Wire

Sharp Curved Manicure Scissors

Gum Arabic Glue

Knot Tamper (Awl)

Bead Board

Wiping Cloth

Yardstick or Ruler

Size AA Stainless Steel Beading Tweezers

French wire is a very fine wire that has been coiled into a hollow flexible tube and must be handled very gently on a smooth surface, or it will snag and pull apart. It is used to conceal and reinforce the exposed thread around the clasp and once you've learned to use it you will find other uses for it in your designing. It is available in gold and silver color, in sizes fine, medium and large.

Having made your self needle and thread, carefully remove the French wire from the box and examine the end to make sure all the wire is coiled, snipping off any wire that is not.

Fig. 1A. Cut off approximately 3/8" of French wire and thread it on to your needle, pulling it down with your thumb and index finger to approximately 2" from the bottom. If you have difficulty feeding one end of the wire on to your needle try the other end. The opening may have closed off in cutting the wire. Next thread the needle through either side of the clasp ring and bring the clasp down above the French wire.

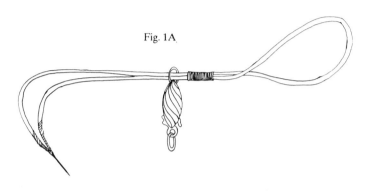

Fig. 1A.

Fig. 1B. Put your needle through the loop at the bottom of the thread, and pull the needle until approximately a 3" circle remains.

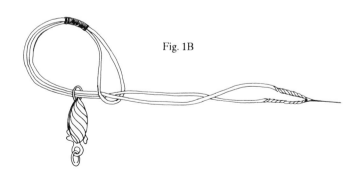

Fig. 1B

Fig. 1C. With thumb and forefinger slide the French wire over to close off the circle.

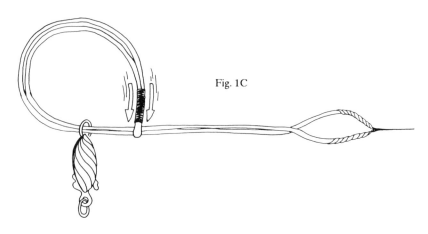

Fig. 1C

Fig. 1D. Hold the clasp down on the table with your left forefinger and with your right hand, pull the needle and thread to bring the loop around the clasp ring. With your thumbnail and index finger push the French wire together to form a ring. This not only conceals the thread around the clasp, but it also strengthens the most vulnerable part of the necklace and is a true hallmark of quality. French wire makes the difference in custom bead stringing.

Fig. 1D

Proceed to string and knot the method of your choice while looking for a bead with a larger hole, saving it for the last bead to be strung. Continue to string until only two beads are left. String them on but do not knot them; the last bead strung is the one with the largest hole.

Fig. 2. Cut off another 3/8" of French wire and thread it on the needle. Thread the needle through the loose ring on the other side of the clasp and back through the hole of the last bead, above the thread already in the bead. (This is the reason we saved a bead with the largest hole for last). It helps to hold the last bead over your left index finger, pulling the thread coming out of each side of the bead down taut to make room for the needle to go through the bead. If your needle is not stiff enough or fine enough to go through the bead, make a new one. Ease the french wire around the clasp ring while pulling the thread through the bead until all the beads are close together and the French wire has formed a circle around the clasp ring.

Fig. 2.

Fig. 3. To finish off, split your needle, making sure your threads are not twisted and the beads are close together, tie a knot and put a dab of gum arabic on it. Holding one thread, reverse the beads and tie another knot on the other side and apply another dab of glue, reverse, tie, and glue again for a total of three knots. Wipe off any excess glue while pulling the knot tight. Let dry for a few minutes until the thread on each side of the bead begins to stiffen. Cut one thread on the side closest to the knot (there is a difference) and then the other. With your knot tamper (awl) tamp the ends into the knot. Put a dab of clear nail polish on the knot to waterproof the closing. By alternating sides when tying and glueing the knots, tamping in the ends of the final one, we end up with a knot that looks like all the others.

Fig. 3.

Fig. 4. If the last bead hole is absolutely too small to accept the needle, then you must split your needle apart before stringing the very last bead. Choosing the best needle of the two threads, moisten and retwist it, (it seldom is necessary to resharpen or reglue it), put the last bead on, then the 3/8" French wire, thread through the clasp ring and put your needle back through the last bead and tie off as above. This is less desirable than using the needle with two threads but the French wire reinforces the thread sufficiently around the clasp ring making it acceptable. Finish tying off as in Fig. 3.

Fig. 4.

I chose to teach the above methods in my video using tweezers to make the knots. It is the easiest way to learn, with only one knot to be tied and glued at the very end, which if done properly, is completely invisible.

In conjunction with the video, I thought it would be a good idea, especially for people with no knowledge of the jewelry industry, to have the tools and beads to enable them to string along with me, so I started to put a kit together. Finding it unfeasible to include the gum arabic I had been using for years, I set off down the path of research, once again asking knowledgeable people "where" and "how to", learning the tricks of the trade and loving the challenge, until they were able to come up with a more perfect gum arabic. One that produces a stiffer needle and is now the only glue specifically made for beading on silk thread! The most wonderful thing about gum arabic is that it is water soluble, washes off tools and beads, is easy to use and the knots can be made waterproof with a simple dab of clear nail polish. It is the only glue that enables you to make a self needle.

Although gum arabic can be used on nylon thread to make a needle I advise using a flexible wire beading needle for such thread. So let's go on to learn how to use one!

Chapter 5: Learning To Attach A Clasp With French Wire Using A Flexible Wire Needle

Materials:

16" 8MM Mother of Pearl Beads

79" Gudebrod Champion White Silk Size FF
or Champion Nylon Size FF Thread

1 Gold Fishhook Clasp

Medium Size Gold French Wire

1 #8 Stainless Steel Flexible Wire Beading Needle

Sharp Curved Manicuring Scissors

Gum Arabic

Knot Tamper (Awl)

Bead Board

Wiping Cloth

Yardstick or Ruler

Size AA Stainless Steel Beading Tweezers

Having explained what French wire is in Chapter 4, let's proceed to learn how to use it with a flexible wire beading needle.

Fig. 1. Thread the silk through the eye of the beading needle, and holding the two ends together, make an over hand knot with your fingers close to the end. String three beads on. Cut 3/8" of French wire and put your needle through it to feed it on the silk. Next, thread the needle through the loose ring on either side of the clasp.

Fig. 1.

Fig. 2. Raise the last bead strung (c) up approximately 2 to 3" above the knot and put the wire needle through bead "c", making sure the needle is above the thread already in the bead. It helps to hold bead "c" over your left index finger while pulling the thread on each side of the bead down taut to allow the needle to pass through without snagging the thread already in the bead, making it impossible to pull the needle through.

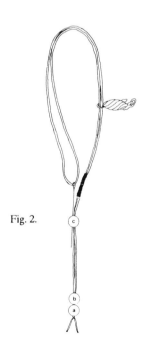

Fig. 2.

Fig. 3. Pull the needle and thread No. 2 all the way through bead "c", easing the French wire around the clasp ring, pushing the French wire closed with bead "c" to form a ring. Making sure the threads are even, tie thread No. 1 and thread No. 2 together in a simple overhand knot.

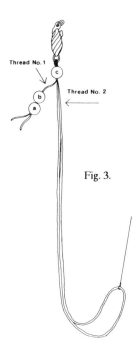

Fig. 3.

Fig. 4. Push bead "b" up to bead "c" bringing the wire needle through bead "b" as in Fig. 2, making sure to pass wire needle above thread already in the bead. Tie thread No. 1 and No. 2 together as in Fig. 3.

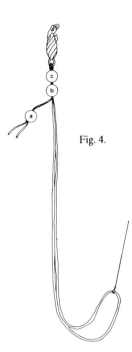

Fig. 4.

Fig. 5. Bring the needle through bead "a", pulling bead "a" down toward the knot on thread No. 1. Paint approximately 1/2" of the four strands of thread coming out of bead "b" above bead "a" with gum arabic, using just enough glue to moisten all the strands of thread.

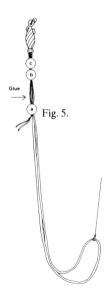

Glue →

Fig. 5.

Fig. 6. Slide bead "a" back to bead "b" and clip thread No. 1 close to the bead hole and knot in front of this bead with tweezer, awl, or fingers. The ends will disappear into the knot if they were clipped close enough. Continue stringing and knotting until only 3 beads are left.

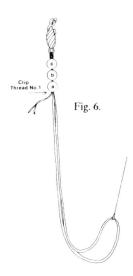

Clip
Thread No. 1 →

Fig. 6.

Fig. 7. String the last three beads on but do not knot these. Put on another 3/8" French wire and thread the needle through the clasp ring of the other side of the clasp.

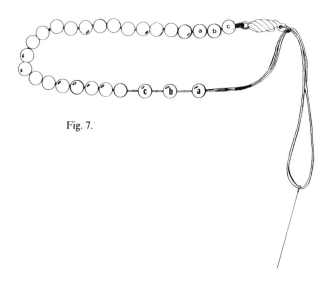

Fig. 7.

Fig. 8. Pass the needle back through bead "a", above the thread already in bead, and pull the needle and thread until the French wire is looped around the clasp ring, making sure all the beads are close together.

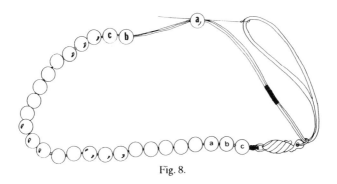

Fig. 8.

Fig. 9. Make a loop on one side of the beads (like an inverted U), and bring the needle and thread around and between bead "a" and bead "b" and up through the loop, pulling the thread to make a knot between bead "a" and "b".

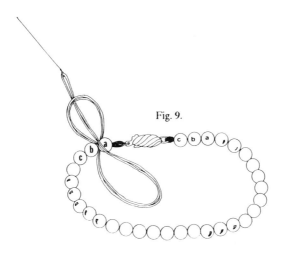

Fig. 9.

Next, (figure not shown) put the needle and thread through the hole of bead "b", keeping needle above thread in bead and repeat making a loop and tying knot between bead "b" and "c".

Fig. 10. Pass the needle through bead "c", above thread already in bead, pulling the thread until approximately a 1 1/2" loop remains. Paint 1/2" of all the threads coming out of bead "b" with gum arabic, and then continue to pull thread all the way through bead "c."

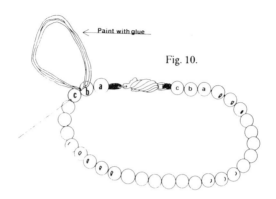

Fig. 10.

Fig. 11. Clip both threads coming out of bead "c" as close to the hole as possible. Paint this knot with clear nail polish to waterproof closing.

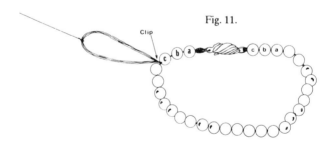

Fig. 11.

As there is no "Beaders Board of Trade" or a "Beaders Vigilance Committee" to set standards for beading, or to hold jewelers accountable for high prices and low quality work, it's up to you to decide which method enables you to acheive professional results by trying them all!

Chapter 6: Learning To Make A Necklace Without A Clasp

Materials:

24" 8MM Mother of Pearl Beads

111" Gudebrod's Champion White Silk Thread Size FF

Sharp Curved Manicuring Scissors

Knot Tamper (Awl)

Wiping Cloth

Bead Board

Yardstick or Ruler

Size AA Stainless Steel Beading Tweezers

Optional: 1 #10 Flexible Wire Beading Needle

A necklace without a clasp is often called an endless necklace. It should be at least 24" to 26" long or large enough to go over your head easily without any stress on the knots, thread or beads. It can be longer if you wish. Remembering the rule of thumb for measuring the thread is four times the length of the unstrung beads, in this case 24", plus 15", or 4 x 24" + 15", cut a piece of thread 111". I prefer a self thread needle as it does not get snagged or tangled on the silk thread as a wire one often does.

Fig. 1. Whether you are using a self needle or a flexible wire one, keeping the two threads even from the needle, tie them together with a simple overhand knot close to the bottom. Before stringing the first bead on, look through the beads for one with a larger hole and string it on the thread first, then put another bead on. Push the two beads down to the knot, and approximately 7" from the first knot tie another overhand knot pulling it tight. Put the next bead on and using the method of your choice to knot, continue to string and knot all but the very last bead.

Fig. 1.

Fig. 2. Put the last bead on and do not knot. Go back to the very first bead strung, holding it over your left index finger, pulling the threads coming out of each side of the bead down taut to make room, put your needle through the bead above the thread already in the bead, pulling the needle thread to the left while pulling the end with the knot to the right until all the beads are close together.

Fig. 2.

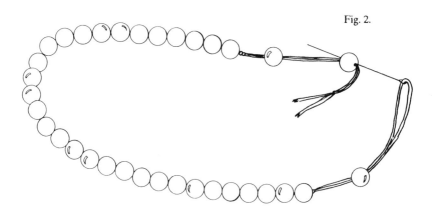

Fig. 3. Leaving approximately 7" of thread from the bead, cut the needle thread off, and open the threads. Making sure they are not twisted, tie them together in an overhand knot with your fingers and put a dab of gum arabic on the knot. Cut the knot off the other thread, opening the threads, making sure they are not twisted, tie and glue. Holding one strand from each knot on the same side of the beads, reverse the beads and tie and glue one knot, then tie and glue the other knot. Holding the two strands on the same side of the beads again, reverse the beads and tie and glue, tie and glue, for a total of three knots. It is important to tie each knot on the opposite side each time to keep the knot small. Wipe the excess glue off while pulling the knots tight. Let dry for a few minutes until the threads near the knot begin to stiffen. Cut each thread on the side closest to the knot, tamping the ends into the knot with your knot tamper (awl). Paint the knots with colorless nail polish to waterproof closing.

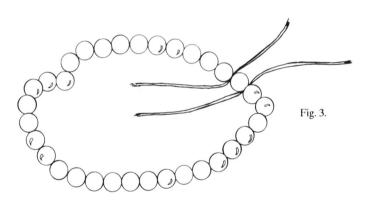

Fig. 3.

That's how to make an endless necklace!

Chapter 7: Pearls

1.   About Pearls

Pearls rank in value with the most precious stones, and the pearl is the only gem that attains perfection in the sea. They are soft and they absorb, as well as, reflect light. They have long been the adornment enhancing a bride's loveliness and reflecting her happiness. Often they're handed down to her by her mother or grandmother on her wedding day. Pearls, whether real or faux, are probably the most important fashion accessory in a woman's wardrobe. Appropriately worn day or night, they are for every occasion.

Natural pearls, extremely rare, are found in certain types of oysters. Cultured pearls are real pearls produced by inserting a mother-of-pearl bead into the tissue of a similar type oyster. The oyster coats this bead with nacre, creating a cultured pearl, and the more coats of nacre the oyster produces the more lustrous and costly the pearl becomes. This process was developed in Japan by Kokichi Mikimoto in the early 1900's.

Pearls are judged by lustre, blemishes, size, shape, color and match. When selecting color, most important is the shade that flatters your skin type. Usually the rose tones are for more fair complexions and the darker shades are for creamy or olive complexions.

The more you wear your pearls the more beautiful they become if they are given proper care. They should be stored in their own pouch or box, out of contact with your other jewelry, so they cannot be scratched. They must be kept free of dirt, body oil, perspiration and cosmetics, especially perfume and hairspray and wiped frequently with a damp cloth. A little known, but most important fact, not publicized by many jewelers at the time of purchase, is that pearls should be cleaned and restrung at least once a year to maintain their lustre.

To make everyone who owns pearls aware of this fact and in my endeavor to introduce pearl and bead stringing as a new American craft and hobby to the general public, I offered to restring the First Lady Barbara Bush's now famous pearls. I suggested to her that after all those long months on the hot dusty campaign trail her pearls, if not already restrung, must surely be in need of restringing to keep them beautiful and lustrous. In reply, I received a letter from the Director of Correspondence for Mrs. Bush stating, "although she will not be able to accept your kind offer, I know Mrs. Bush would want me to thank you for writing to her." When pearls are worn as often as Mrs. Bush wears hers, they must be restrung two or three times a year. Although I was not allowed the privilege of performing this service for her, I do hope the First Lady was informed as to their care, for only then will they become an heirloom handed down from generation to generation.

2. Styles and Lengths of Necklaces

Graduated - A necklace of graduated size beads with the largest at the center, decreasing in size on each side towards the clasp.

Uniform - All the pearls are within 1/2 MM of each other in size.

Choker - One or more strands worn just above the collar-bone.

Princess - 18" length

Matinee - 22" to 24" in length

Opera - 30" to 32" in length

Bib - A necklace with many strands, each one longer that the one above it.

Rope - 45" or longer, sometimes called a lariat or sautoir.

3.   How to Clean and Restring Pearls

When restringing cultured pearls they should be cleaned while still strung on the old thread with mild soap, such as Ivory Flakes, in lukewarm water. Using a soft cloth, remove any dirt and body oil that have collected around the drill hole on each side of the pearl. The safest way to do this is to place a collander, lined with a turkish hand towel in the sink. Keep the drain closed to ensure that no pearls will be lost if the weakened thread breaks. Then rinse them extremely well to make sure no soap residue remains to dull or harm their lustre. Let them dry over night before cutting them apart.

Refer back to Chapter 1 to find the proper way to cut knotted beads apart. It is a good idea, as you cut them apart, to line them up on your bead board in the order they were strung, especially if they are graduated and more than one strand, to facilitate restringing. A millimeter gauge is a helpful tool when stringing pearls. If the clasp is not the centerpiece of the necklace and is worn at the back, the more imperfect pearls are placed nearest to it. Pearls are always strung on silk thread and the clasp attached with French wire. The correct size silk thread for 6 MM and larger pearls is E, size D for 4 and 5 MM, and C or B for the very tiniest holed pearls.

Chapter 8: Learning To Weave Beads

1. *How to Make a Woven Bracelet*
2. *How to Make a Woven Lariat*

1.   How to Make a Woven Bracelet

Materials:

73-82 - 4mm round beads for 7" bracelet

1 - 5 1/2 MM Spring ring clasp

1 - 5 MM Soldered jump ring

Gudebrod's 6 lb. test clear Gem Monofilament

Crystal cement

Sharp curved scissor

Ruler

Size AA Stainless Steel Beading Tweezers

Fig. 1. Cut approximately 36" of the monofilament and bring the two ends together. Feed both ends through the soldered jump ring part of the clasp and then back between the two strands on the other side of the ring, pulling to bring the loop tight around the clasp ring.

Fig. 1.

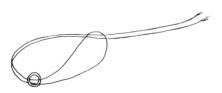

Fig. 2. String both ends through a bead and with your tweezer make a knot next to the bead. Open the strands to tighten the knot, but don't pull too tightly. String two beads on the left strand, the second bead strung will be the center bead of the bracelet. Put one bead on the right hand strand. The right hand strand will act as your needle.

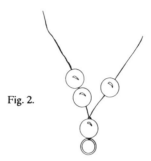

Fig. 2.

Fig. 3. Put the right strand down through the top hole of the bead on the left hand strand, and pull the two strands towards you to bring the beads together. By moving the center bead, adjust the strands to center the two beads directly between the first bead strung. Continue stringing and each time you have strung three or four sets of beads on, go back to tighten the beads. Start with the first set strung and push the center bead forward of each set strung with your thumbnail. Work until desired length, allowing for the width of the clasp, and go back to the beginning and tighten all the beads again before ending off, to ensure that all the beads are tight.

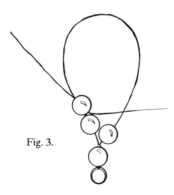

Fig. 3.

Fig. 4. To finish off, string one bead on each strand and tie the two strands together with your fingers in a double knot. Make sure the knot is centered between the two beads.

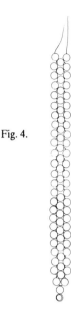

Fig. 4.

Fig. 5. Put the two strands through the last bead, then through the soldered spring ring and back through the last bead. Tie the two strands together with you fingers and pull the knot tight. Reverse the bracelet and tie again on the other side for a total of two knots. Cut the ends close to the knot and put a drop of crystal cement on the knots to fuse them together.

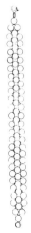

Fig. 5.

This is a lovely bracelet that's so easy to make taking only an hour or so. It can be as inexpensive or as expensive as you like with beautiful results in any instance. It can be enhanced using contrasting or gold beads. Create diagonal stripes, flowers in a row, a stripe of gold beads down the center, or just use a few gold beads in the middle. To give this bracelet a totally different look, use a 4x5 fresh water pearl for the center bead.

Originally, I made this bracelet on silk thread with lapis lazuli and gold beads, attaching the clasp with French wire, using a self needle, twisting and splitting and retwisting the needle as needed. It was an exact copy of one I had seen in an elegant Fifth Avenue jewelry store, whose name you would know, retailing for more than seven times my cost to make! It did not hold up very well, and I had to keep restringing it until I found this excellent soft monofilament which can be successfully knotted and tied with more lasting results.

Recently Gudebrod, Inc. developed C-Thru-B Translucent Cord which works even better in some instances, and I'll show you how to use it next!

2.   How to Make a Woven Lariat

Materials:

Approximately 600 - 4MM diamond shaped Austrian Crystals for a 40-45" Lariat

Approximately 72 - 6 MM round crystals

4 - 10 MM diamond shaped crystals

2 - 90" strands of Gudebrod's fine size C-THRU-B Translucent Cord

2 - #8 stainless steel flexible wire needles

Crystal cement

Sharp curved scissors

Size A Stainless Steel Beading Tweezers

Ruler or yardstick

To make a lariat, we'll use C-Thru-B translucent cord. This necklace can be made with less difficulty using the monofilament used in making the woven bracelet because you don't need to use beading needles. However, it is well worth the extra bother of using beading needles with this special cord when you see the results. The necklace will be as supple as if it were strung on silk thread, and it will be even stronger, with less stretch, then if it were strung on monofilament. However, because the ends are too soft, you must use beading needles. To keep from having to rethread the needle each time, I use one on each end. As we work on, I'll give you hints as to how to keep the needles from falling off. This necklace is worked in two sections and joined at the back. It is a variation of the weave in the bracelet.

Fig. 1. Take one of the 90" of the cord and thread it through a flexible wire needle and string 4 - 4 MM beads on, bringing them down to the center of the cord (center from end to end).

Fig. 1.

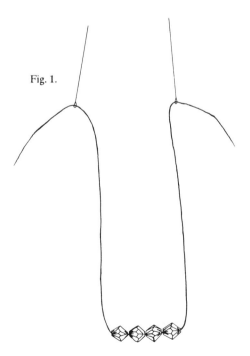

Fig. 2. Put the right hand needle down into the top hole of the first bead strung.

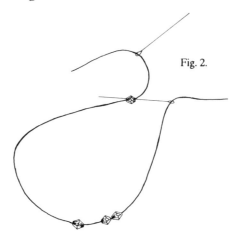

Fig. 2.

Fig. 3. Pull both strands toward you to bring the beads together. Adjust the beads and cord to form a diamond shape. Put a needle on the left hand cord.

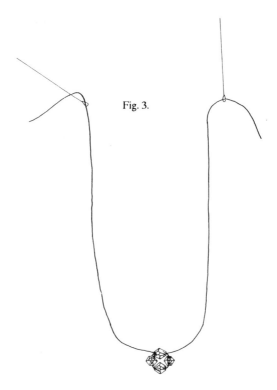

Fig. 3.

Fig. 4. String a 10 MM bead on with the left strand needle and then put the right strand needle through the same bead.

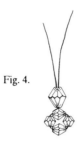

Fig. 4.

Fig. 5. With your tweezers make a knot in front of the bead and open strands to tighten the knot, but don't pull too tightly. String another 10 MM bead on in the same manner and knot again.

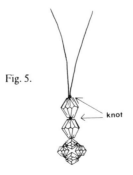

Fig. 5.

knot

Fig. 6. String four 4 MM beads on the right hand needle. *HINT: Don't pull them down beyond the two strands, but just far enough to lock on the needle.* String four 4 MM beads on the left needle and one 6 MM round bead and pull them all the way down. *HINT: Put something small and heavy on top of this needle and cord to keep the needle from falling off.* Go back to the right hand needle and pull the beads down and put the needle down into the top of the round bead on the left strand.

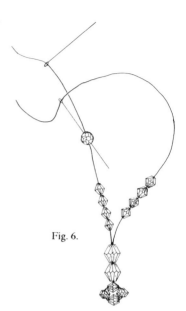

Fig. 6.

Fig. 7. Pull both strands towards you.

Fig. 7.

Fig. 8. Repeat the sequence of four 4 MM beads on the right strand and four 4 MM and one 6 MM on the left strand, tightening after 4 or 5 sets are strung by pushing on center (round) bead, as we did making the bracelet, for approximately 22", ending with only two 4 MM beads on each strand. Go back to Fig. 1 and repeat for second half of necklace, ending off with two 4 MM beads on each strand.

Fig. 8.

Fig. 9. The graphic shows how the top half of the necklace looks completed. Both the top and bottom strands are ended off the same way. Remove the left hand needle and match the two necklaces at the back. Take the right hand needle from the right bottom half of the necklace and put it through the last bead of the bottom half of the left side of the necklace, pulling the cord ends of both necklaces in opposite directions to bring the beads together. Remove the needle and tie each cord separately by making a loop on one side of the necklace. Bring the cord around

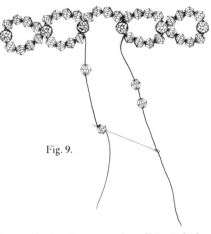

Fig. 9.

between the two beads and back through the loop and pull it tightly as shown in Fig. 9, Chapter 5. Do this twice. Repeat with the other cord. Cut each cord close to the knot and apply a drop of crystal cement on each knot. The crystal cement will fuse the knots together. Let dry and repeat with the bottom half of necklace.

Alternate closing: if you are having difficulty keeping the beads tightly together on the cord or monofiliment when tying off, you may simply tie the matching strands together in a double overhead knot with your fingers. Reverse the necklace and tie third knot. Clip the strands close to the knot and apply crystal cement.

I have named this my "Thousand Points of Light" necklace because, literally, thousands of lights do bounce off the points of the crystals like tiny little dancing rainbows.

One of my former students, turned entrepreneur, made her lariat to wear to a wedding, and it was such a show stopper, she received countless compliments and six orders for the necklace. Though it's more sparkling in crystal, it has a beautifully subdued elegance when made in stone beads. Weaving works best using 4 MM beads. You will need approximately seven 16" strands of 4 MM round beads, figuring 100 - 4 MM beads come on a 16" strand. You may vary the design by using more or less beads in each set, with perhaps a tassel of beads at each end, but I'll leave that to your imagination. So you want to know more? Let's go on to more!

Chapter 9: More Baubles Bangles and Beads

If you have learned to do all the things in articles 1, 2, 3 and 4 of Chapter 3, completed Chapter 4 and are able to do the endless necklace closing in Chapter 6, you will have no difficulty mastering this chapter. When you have done this, you will be able to look at any necklace and know how it was strung, and you will be well on your way to designing and stringing an individually styled piece of jewelry!

1. How to Use Bead Tips

Very heavy beads or some ethnic metal beads that cannot be strung on chain, or if you do not wish to string on chain, can be strung on jewelry wire. This is sometimes called tiger tail and is attached to the clasp with bead tips. There are two types of bead tips, the clam and the cup. It is best to use the clam type on tiger tail as it conceals the sharp ends of the wire completely and looks like a little gold or silver bead when closed.

Fig. 1. Choose a size wire strong enough to support your beads, and cut the length needed, allowing approximately 10" to tie the knots. Tie two or three knots, depending on the size wire used, one on top of the other with your fingers, and use your chain nose plier to pull the knots tight. Clip the excess wire off close to the knots, and put a drop of crystal cement on them.

Fig. 1.

Fig. 2. Place the knots in the bead tip, fitting the wire coming from the knot into the groove of the bead tip, and squeeze the clam shut with a chain nose plier.

Fig. 2.

Fig. 3. After all the beads are strung, make a knot close to the last bead strung using your tweezer, just as you did between the beads on the silk thread. Push the knot close to the bead with you tweezer. Repeat this, placing one knot on top of the other, as you did on the other side. Cut off the excess wire and put a drop of crystal cement on the knot and place it in the bead tip. Fit the wire the beads are strung on into the groove of the bead tip, and squeeze it closed with the chain nose plier. Some beaders find it easier to place the knot in the bead tip before cutting the excess wire, cutting the wire after the bead tip is closed. If you do this, you must be very careful to cut  the wire very close to the bead tip.

Fig. 3.

Fig. 4. Attach the bead tip to the clasp by twisting one side of the bead tip ring opening either forward or backward to open it. Place it on the clasp and then twist it closed in the opposite direction you opened it to close it back to its original position. If the bead tip has a hook end, roll it closed around the clasp or clasp ring with a round nose plier.

Fig. 4.

2. How To Use Bead Crimps

Bead crimps are tiny hollow tubes usually used on more rigid monofilament that cannot be knotted, such as ordinary fishing line.

Fig. 1. Feed one end of the strand through the bead crimp, then through the clasp ring and back through the crimp. Leave enough filament on the short strand to go through the first two or three beads. Bring the crimp next to the clasp ring and flatten it by squeezing it with a chain nose plier locking the monofilament onto the clasp. String the first two or three beads on with the double strand to hide the end.

Fig. 1.

Fig. 2. To end, feed a crimp on the strand and put the strand through the other side of the clasp ring and back through the crimp. Feed the strand through two or three beads, pulling the beads close together until the crimp is against the clasp. Flatten the crimp and cut off the excess filament close to the bead hole.

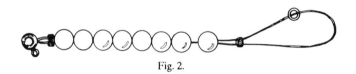

Fig. 2.

3.   How To String a Two or More Strand Bracelet

To string a two or more strand bracelet, you need a clasp with as many rings and separaters with as many holes as you have strands. Each strand is strung individually, one at a time, just as you would string a necklace using silk thread and French wire to attach the clasp. All the strands are the same length and the separaters are strung in their respective holes off center to hold the strands together. The 7 inch bracelet shown here has two decorative diamond separaters towards the center of the bracelet with one plain one on each side. There are 2 inches between the two diamond separaters in the middle and 1 1/8 inch on either side of the plain separaters for a total of 6 1/2 inches. Including 1/2 inch for the clasp, which must be counted as part of the bracelet, we have 7 inches, the standard size for a bracelet. For a two or three strand bracelet, two separater bars are usually enough and are placed approximately 2 inches from the clasp on each side.

If your clasp does not have a safety lock, you can buy a ready made safety chain with a spring ring on one end and a tiny jump ring on the other end. This is put on while the first row is being strung. After the clasp is attached and the first bead strung is knotted, put the jump ring on and continue to bead and knot. The spring ring hangs loose until the strand has been completed and attached between the last two beads. Make sure the safety chain opens on the same side as the clasp.

4.   How To Make a Tassel

A tassel of beads may be used as a decoration on either side of a lariat or as a center piece of a necklace and is usually made of 2 - 3 or 4 MM beads. The one shown here is a four strand one. You can make yours as many strands and as long as you like, but you must have something wide enough to cover the knot that ties them together. In this case, a gold rondel with a large hole was sufficient. There are tassel covers that come in various sizes of gold or silver and large enough to fit over multiple strands covering the knot, like this one shown next to the tassel.

Start the first strand by making a self needle at one end of a single strand of thread, either stringing a 2 or 3 MM gold bead on the strand and then, bringing the two ends together, make a new needle and string on a stone 4 MM bead. If you don't have a gold bead you can use French wire to close off the bead hole. Cut 1/8" piece of French wire and proceed the same way, and it will look like a gold bead. It is not necessary to cut all the thread as long as the necklace will be, just the ones that will be used to continue on with the necklace on each side after the tassel is complete. The tassel shown here was used as a pendant and the necklace was worked from either side of it. I made two short threads about 30" long for two strands of the tassel and two longer ones, using enough thread to make each side of the necklace. When the four tassels are completed, you may find it easier to hold all the strands evenly, and knot them together with your tweezer as if you were making a knot between a bead. Then separate the strands evenly, and tie them together again using your fingers, glueing after each knot with Gum Arabic. Cut the short strands off, tamping in the ends, and apply clear nail polish to waterproof the knots. Passing both needles through, string on the cover bead and perhaps a bead rondel, a small gold bead and finally a large bead to complete the tassel. Knot this bead and continue on to complete each side of the necklace separately, ending with or without a clasp.

5. How To Attach a Dragon Clasp

This is an inexpensive and popular clasp that is worn to the side, adding a stunning accent to a necklace and it comes in a variety of semi-precious stones. It is beautifully attached with French wire, concealing and strengthening the thread around the clasp. The necklace is worked in two pieces and joined at the back. The ring is the top part of the necklace and should be about 8 1/2" long including the ring.

Fig. 1. Cut 47" of thread and make a self needle. Attach the ring in the manner we learned to attach a clasp. Feed enough French wire on your needle to go around the **_narrowest_** part of the ring tightly. Refer back to Chapter 4 for directions on how to attach a clasp. String on, and knot enough beads until it measures 8 1/2" including the last two beads, which you do not knot, and the ring.

Fig. 1.

Fig. 2. To work the bottom part of the necklace, determine the length you want the neclace to be, remembering to count the 8 1/2" into the length, and make a thread needle. This is attached a little differently than a regular clasp as the french wire will probably not go through the hole, so follow along. Cut enough French wire to go from the hole around to the bottom of the clasp on one side. You may have to experiment with the size of the wire. Feed it onto your needle bringing it down to approximately 2" from the bottom and put the needle through the hole at the bottom part of the dragon clasp, and bring that down above the French wire. Put another piece of French wire on, the same size as the first piece, above the clasp. Put the needle through the loop, and slide the French wire that you strung on first over to close off the loop. Make sure the second piece of French wire is within the circle. Pull the needle thread, closing the French wire around both sides of the clasp, and push the wire together. Continue to bead and knot for the desired length until one bead is left. Follow the directions in Chapter 6 for an endless necklace closing to complete.

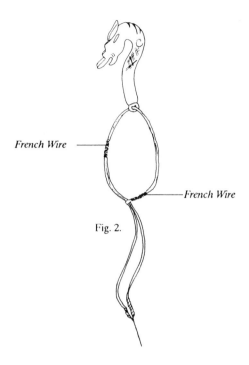

French Wire

French Wire

Fig. 2.

Fig. 3. You must be very careful putting the ring around the dragon's neck to connect the clasp. It must be done in this fashion: slip the narrowest part of the ring under the dragon's neck and slide the ring around to bring the thickest part of the ring under the dragon's neck. This locks the ring onto the dragon and it will not come off when the necklace is worn. Never force the ring over the dragon's head as you may snap his head off. Simply turn the ring to bring the narrowest part under his neck to remove it over his head easily.

Fig. 3.

6.   How To Use a One Strand Clasp For a Two Strand Necklace

Two strands of beads may be strung on a one strand clasp as long as it is strong enough to support the two strands. Sometimes the clasp ring is not large enough to allow the second piece of French wire to go through, so we must cut the wire in half and string a piece on each side of the ring. When the French wire is pushed together, it looks just like the first strand. Follow the directions for Fig. 2 of the dragon clasp to attach.

7.   How To Attach a Front to Back Hole Pendant

This figure is a little Oriental lady side accent piece which usually has a hole going through the entire length of the piece from top to bottom. However, this lady has a hole on top of her head which comes out through the back of her head at the top. This necklace must be strung in two pieces with the top piece being 8 1/2" long. The French wire must be put on in two pieces as shown in the drawing, just as we did the dragon clasp. With the first piece of wire on, put the needle down into the top of the head, and bring it out through the back hole. You may use your tweezer to help pull the needle through. Put the next piece of French wire on and follow the direction for Fig. 2 of the dragon clasp. The bottom part of the necklace is attached in the same manner, by putting the needle through the bottom hole and bringing it out the back to complete the necklace.

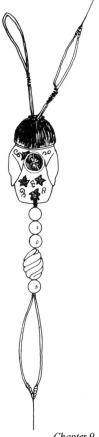

8. How To Attach a Pendant With a Hole at the Top

Cut a strand of thread the desired length of the necklace, and bring the two ends together to make a self needle. Cut the thread at the other end, and make another self needle. Feed a piece of French wire on large enough to go from the hole to the top of the pendant, and bring it down to the center of the thread. Put the pendant on and then another piece of French wire the same size, and bring them to the center. Put both needles through the hole of a bead larger than the ones being used for the necklace. If you are using 8 MM beads, use a 10 MM bead, etc. Use the bead to push the wire together around the hole of the pendant. With your tweezer, make a knot next to the bead, and open the threads to tighten the knot. Continue on, working each side of the necklace separately.

9.   How To Attach a Pendant With a Ring of Beads

The pendant pictured can be attached with French wire just as we did the bottom part of the dragon clasp or the Oriental lady, or you can attach it with a ring of beads as shown here. Work each side of the necklace in the following manner: cut the proper size thread for one half of the necklace, and make a thread needle using only one end of the thread. Thread the amount of 2 -3 or 4 MM beads for half the size of the loop. Put the pendant on and then the beads for the other half of the loop. Bringing the two threads from each side of the pendant together to even the two threads, tie the ring of beads together with your fingers in a double knot, making sure there is no slack between the beads. You may use your tweezers to make the knot, and then open the threads to tighten the knot. Bring the two threads together, and make a new needle. Continue on with your design to complete the necklace.

10.   How To Make a Two or More Strand Necklace

When making a double, triple or more strand necklace, each strand should be 1/2" longer than the one above. Before closing the second strand, put the needle and thread through the clasp ring, and try it on to see how much lower or higher you want it. I recommend you do this for each ensuing row because a fraction of a millimeter difference in the size of beads can throw the necklace off.

11.   How To Make a Twisted Necklace

When making a multi-strand twisted necklace all the strands are strung the same length. Allow an additional 1 to $1^{1/2}$" on each strand for a thick necklace to get the desired length. Example: if you want your necklace to be 16", make all the strands 17 to $17^{1/2}$", according to the thickness of the twist. The strands are twisted before the necklace is put on. You cannot make a twisted necklace without a clasp.

12.   How To Enhance Dull Stone Beads

Some more porous stone beads that have lost their luster can be enhanced by rubbing the tiniest drop of mineral oil between the palms of your hands and fingers and then rubbing them over and around the bead. This sometimes brings out qualities you did not see in the beads before. However, if you put too much oil on you will have to rub the beads dry and restring them.

13.   How To Use a Pearl Shortener to Change the Style of Your Beads

If you make an endless necklace 30" or more you can make it into a 15" or longer two strand necklace by using a pearl shortener such as the one shown. This endless necklace has six design stations with six beads separating each station. By inserting the pearl shortener between the two strands in the middle of the six beads on one side, then the other, I have a beautiful two strand necklace with the designs matching on each strand.

In order to do this, you must use an even amount of design stations, spaced evenly on the necklace.

14.   Design Stations

A design station can be a single different bead or a group of beads spaced apart on a necklace or bracelet. It is best not to knot the beads in the station to make the design stand out from the other beads. For example, if you were putting six beads between each station, you would knot five beads, put the sixth bead on without knotting it, string your design, and end it by putting the first bead on of the six beads before knotting again. 14Kt. Gold beads are very often used in designing, and you never knot before or after a 14Kt. gold bead because they are soft and damage easily. They come in three weights, economy, regular and heavy. I do not recommend using economy or light weight 14Kt. gold beads as they dent and crumple very easily.

15.   Attaching an Accent Piece With Rings on Each Side

Many jewelry accent pieces are specifically made to have beads strung from them. The rings can be stationary ones soldered to the back of the piece where they do not show, and the piece is usually made for a two or three strand necklace 16 - 18" in length with a clasp in the back. You always start the necklace at the centerpiece, attaching the thread with French wire to the rings as you would a clasp, and work back towards the clasp, which of course is fastened with French wire. Be sure the clasp is attached on the proper sides of the necklace to facilitate putting it on.

16.   How To Make a Ball Bead Earring

To make ball bead earrings you need two half-drilled beads and a post earring with a peg and cup to fit the size bead you chose. Bring the bead with you when you purchase this finding to make sure the bead fits on the peg and cup properly. Being very careful not to get any glue on your fingers, apply a few drops of Krazy glue to the peg and cup and place the bead hole on the peg and hold them together for a few minutes. I do this easily by pressing the post on the earring into a sheet of styrofoam so I don't have to hold it, ensuring I won't glue my fingers together. I then take a small wad of jeweler's wax molded around a lollipop stick, like a Q-tip, and press the top side of the bead on the wax and practice fitting it on the peg before glueing. When you are sure the bead is set right put the Krazy glue, or other similar epoxy on the peg and cup, and fit the bead on. Hold it there for a few minutes before removing the wax from the bead. That's all there is to making a pair of ball earrings!

17.   How To Make a Hanging Earring

Follow the diagrams. String your pattern of beads on the head pin and bend it down at the bead hole to the right, using your chain nose plier to do this. Cut off all but 1/4" of the wire with your side cutting diagonal wire cutter. Take your round nose plier, and place the end of the wire between the tips of it, and roll the wire around with the plier to the left to form a loop. Buy a bag of inexpensive base metal head pins, and practice this step before using gold or silver ones. Place the loop on any one of the earrings shown below. Remember, the proper way to open the ring of the earring is to twist it forward or backward with your chain nose plier. Place the head pin loop on the ring, and then twist the ring closed in the opposite direction you opened it to close it back to its original position.

18. How To Make a Carved Stone Earring

This square stone has been carved into a basket weave pattern and as the back is flat, it can be made into an earring simply by gluing this post earring with a pad, as shown, to the back of the stone.

I put a dab of jewelry epoxy in the center of the stone and pressed the pad to the stone. Many stones are carved into different shapes and sizes suitable for earrings. Most carved stones are inexpensive, some as low as a dollar each.

19. How To Make a Pin Into a Removable Centerpiece of a Short Necklace.

The center picture below is an old TRIFARI bird pin purchased in the early 1940's. In order to be able to wear the pin as the centerpiece of a short necklace without defacing it, which would decrease it's antiquity value, I use the pin converters shown on either side of the pin.

The pair pictured on the left was used to string fourteen strands of tiny fresh water pearls, all 18" in length from one curved bar to the other. The pair on the right has rings for three strands of beads. Each strand may be longer than the one above it strung from ring to ring or all the same length if you wish to twist them.

I once took a basic beginners jewelry course because I simply wanted to learn to solder a clasp to a chain. Although I did learn to do this, what I learned best was that this was not my forte and is better left for my jeweler to do. When asking your jeweler to make or do something for you, it will cost you less if you buy all the components and bring them to him saving him time. In this case, all he had to do was cut and solder, making this an inexpensive project.

I took the pin to a findings house and purchased silver tubing that fit over the pin stem and a length as long as the stem plus enough extra to make the curved bars. For the pair on the right, I just bought enough tubing to fit over the pin stem and six small jump rings. By making the converter in two pieces it is not necessary to use a clasp.

The necklace is put on in this manner: I twist all the strands of pearls and slip one converter on the pin stem. When the pearls are twisted the necklace is 16$^{1/2}$" long. Holding the pin stem and pin at my neck, I bring the pearls around the back of my neck to the front and slide the other converter onto the pin stem and close the safety lock of the pin.

By using a ring shortener between the two converters, I can wear the necklace as a plain twisted choker.

Of course your pin must be large enough to conceal the converters.

20. Dramatic Effect With 34" Ropes and Ring Shortener

The dramatic center knot necklace in Fig. 3 is made with four 34" endless necklaces as shown in Fig. 1.

Separate the necklaces into pairs and double each pair to make a four strand necklace as in Fig. 2. Overlap strands and pull ends through as indicated by the arrows, pulling each end to form a knot. Attach a ring shortener to hold the necklaces together at the back as shown in Fig. 3.

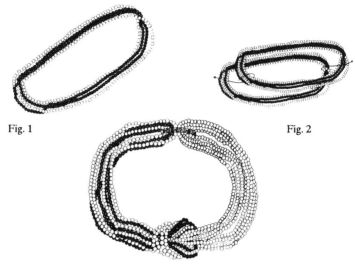

Fig. 1   Fig. 2

Fig. 3

The two tone effect necklace in Fig. 3 was made by pairing a 4 MM rose quartz strand with a garnet strand on one side and two 4 MM crystal strands on the other side. The knot ends up with three colors in it.

Another look can be acheived with this necklace by holding all the strands together at each end and twisting the beads into a lovely rope choker which is clasped at the back with the ring shortener.

21. Selecting the Correct Thread Size

I'd like to say a word about selecting the correct size thread for different kinds of beads, as that is the most frequent question asked of me. Unfortunately, there is no set size for a particular kind or size of stone bead as the drill holes vary. Unlike cultured pearls whose drill holes are consistent because most of them come from Japan, (although that may change as more and more countries are pearl farming), stone bead holes are not consistent in size. Study the drill holes and you will eventually come to know the proper size thread to use for that hole.

22. Number of Beads in 16" Lengths

Most beads come in 15" to 16" length strands strung on nylon filament. Here is a table for the approximate number of beads in a 16" strand although it may vary if the beads are a fraction larger or smaller.

16" Lengths:

Size of Bead	*Number of Beads*
2 MM	218
3 MM	124
4 MM	100
5 MM	80
6 MM	60
7 MM	56
8 MM	50
9 MM	45
10 MM	40
11 MM	36
12 MM	33

23. About Beads

Every culture of the world has used beads for centuries, be they prayer beads, worry beads, monetary beads or beads of adornment. I know of no other hobby that allows you so much freedom of expression or gives such satisfaction for so little time or effort.

You will find beading relaxing, relieving tension and stress. Most of all, it is a very enjoyable experience!

Chapter 10: Sources

If your interest has been sparked enough to want to learn the fine art of pearl and bead stringing, then you will need to buy some tools and beads to get started. As this revolutionary new craft industry is catching on, (and I say "revolutionary new craft industry" because you no longer have to go to a jewelry school charging hundreds of dollars to learn), bead shops have been opening up all over the country. However, you may have to purchase yours from a jewelry findings house or bead supply company.

In most large cities, there are wholesale diamond and jewelry districts servicing retail jewelers. Among these jewelry stores and exchanges are many findings houses that give over-the-counter service to small manufacturers and jewelers in the area. They sell everything from gold and silver sheets and wire to all the component parts along with tools and supplies that go into jewelry making. They also sell retail and wholesale. Look in the yellow pages or your phone directory under jewelry findings or lapidary or bead supplies.

Another source, and probably the easiest for the novice beader, are lapidary magazines. The ones I am familiar with are **_Lapidary Journal_**, **_Rock and Gem_**, **_Ornament_**, and **_Bead and Button_**. You may find them on newsstands, in some public libraries, bead stores and at rock and gem shows.

A visit to a rock and gem show can be quite a fascinating, educational and enjoyable experience for the whole family. This is the very best place to get to know what is available in the market place, with many vendors there looking for your business. Here you can learn all about the different stones, comparing quality and price, and you can take advantage of special show prices by buying on the spot.

Upcoming shows are listed well in advance each month in **_Lapidary Journal_** and **_Rock and Gem_**, allowing you time to plan to attend one. Many of them may be found advertised in the pages of your Sunday newspaper.

If you intend to start a small business, I strongly suggest you apply for a sales tax resale certificate from the state division of taxation which will give you access to all the wonderful wholesale bead supply houses. Some information and advice may be obtained from your state's "*Division of Development for Small Business and Women and Minority Businesses*" office or from your own accountant. This should help you get started.

In the "**Consumer Information Catalog**" printed by the General Services Administration of the Federal Government, available for $1.00, many helpful catalogs are listed under the "Small Business Section", including a 48 page booklet called "*Starting and Managing a Buiness From Your Home*" #114V for $2.00. If you would like a copy of both or just #114V, send $3.00 or $2.00 to S. James, Consumers Information Center-L, P.O. Box 100, Pueblo, CO 81002. Include, along with your requests by name and number, your name and address. If you only want the "**Consumers Information Catalog**" send your request along with $1.00 to R. Woods at the same address.

For those looking for marketing ideas, as well as business management tips, there is a news monthly for craft professionals called **_The Crafts Report_**, P.O. Box 1992, Wilmington, DE 19899, which I can recommend. Craft shows are listed in advance each month, state by state, that you might be interested in attending to decide if you would like to become a vendor at one of them. Speak to some of the vendors there and tell them what you do and that you are thinking of selling at this particular show. Very often they will tell you if it has been a good show for them and may offer information on other shows. Crafters are usually very willing to help each other.

If you have decided to start a company and are thinking about advertising in any publication, you need only call or write to the newspaper or magazine asking for their "Media Kit", and they will send you a copy of their publication along with the cost of different size ads, free of charge.

If you decide you would like to place an ad, before doing so, ask if they have remnant space. This means you may purchase any unsold advertising space at a great discount.

Never be afraid to ask questions, explore your options, or take small risks you can afford. There are always people eager to help you become successful as it sometimes ensures their own success!

Chapter 11: How To Start A Business

It's so easy to earn extra money with your newly acquired skills. It takes very little effort and capital to get started, and you can watch your profits grow quickly as you reinvest and work up to a very lucrative business.

I tell my students the beautiful necklaces they designed will sell right off their necks, and over and over again, they come back to tell me that's exactly how they got started in their business. When you design with precious and semi-precious stone beads, you are making real jewelry just like they sell in fine stores. Only their prices are much higher than what your price would be.

In a guest appearance, on Regis Philbin's live morning T.V. talk show on A.B.C. television, in New York City, I showed the audience a necklace I had purchased the day before in a world famous department store selling for $150, which to my disappointment happened to be marked down to $75.00 that day for a one day Veterans Day sale. I bought the identical black onyx and 14Kt gold beads and showed the viewers how they could duplicate the necklace for $22. After my segment of the show, during a commercial break, Regis told me their hotline was ringing off the hook with callers wanting to know where to buy my video. I was deluged with phone calls and letters for a long time after that, not only from people who wished to learn the art of pearl and bead stringing, but from people wanting to buy my finished necklaces. Everyone loves a bargain and you will be able to give them one. That's why it's so easy to sell.

For those of you who seriously want to build a business, here are a few things you can do to get started. First of all, have some business cards printed stating the services you render, and carry them with you at all times. Next, make yourself a half dozen necklaces of various stones to flatter your wardrobe, using the compliments you receive to advertise that you custom design and make precious and semi-precious necklaces, bracelets and earrings, selling for much less than the retail price. When making your own pieces, if gold beads are included, it might be a wise investment to use 14Kt gold ones. There is something magical about the words "14Kt gold", probably because it denotes real as opposed to costume jewelry.

You will be surprised how inexpensively you can purchase 14Kt gold beads, especially the 3 and 4 MM ones. But when someone asks you the price, be sure you are able to quote it with 14Kt gold filled beads as well, as there is a big difference in the cost. Have a necklace made up with gold filled beads so they can see there is no visible difference in the appearance of either kind should they want to spend less. If you comparison shop stores, you will know how to price your items. One advantage of using 14Kt. gold filled beads is that they do not dent as 14Kt. gold ones do.

Those of you who work in large offices, where women dress up every day, have a market ready to be tapped. If gifts are given on special occasions, let your co-workers know they can give a more expensive gift without spending any more money by letting you custom design something special for the recipient. Make "wearing beads" your trademark to remind people of your talent. Women, as well as men, will be fascinated with your collection of beads and will eventually want you to make something for them to wear or to give as a gift. One of my students, an executive secretary in a large brokerage house with many affluent co-workers, had to teach her mother and sister how to string to help keep up with her orders.

A teacher who took my course is doing extremely well selling to others on staff in her school. She expanded her business when she sold necklaces to two teachers, in two different schools, who started bringing her orders from their schools. In appreciation, she made each of them a necklace as a gift and eventually worked out a system by which they accumulated credit to purchase more expensive pieces. Sometimes she even pays them a cash commission. When people know they can earn money, or get a piece of jewelry by helping someone to save money, you'll be surprised at their enthusiasm to sell for you.

Let me tell you how Anne got started. On a visit to a dress shop catering to the taller woman, where she buys her clothes, she showed the proprieter the necklace she was wearing and said she had designed it herself and finally has beads that are long enough for her height. The owner agreed that her customers also needed longer necklaces and Anne, seizing the opportunity, suggested she make up some for her to sell with a money back guarantee if they did not. The owner was delighted, and they looked through the stock to see which outfits could be enhanced with a necklace.

Involving the owner in the designing made it more challenging, giving her more incentive to suggest *her* designs to customers. Anne never had to give any money back and, with her confidence boosted, was able to sell her pieces to other boutique shops. Anne also attaches a little hand painted signature card tied with a ribbon to each piece. She notes the kind of stones and gold used, giving them the designer touch and thus establishing her identity.

Then there were two friends who learned to bead from my video and decided to pool their work and sell at craft shows, sharing the expenses. Many of the shows they entered were juried. This means the sponsors only accept the artisans chosen by a panel of jurors who examine slides or photos of their work to see if it is exceptional enough or suitable for their show. It was after a particularly disappointing show in November, one that was touted to bring thousands of Christmas buyers to them, that I met one of the young ladies at a jewelry findings house in New York City. She recognized me from my video, introduced herself and proceeded to tell me her tale of woe. I invited her out to lunch and told her I had a solution for them and that the timing was perfect. I suggested she and her friend immediately send out invitations to all their customers for an open house jewelry party to be held in her home. They invited friends, relatives, neighbors, their children's school teachers, and anyone else they could think of who might be a Christmas shopper. They added a note at the bottom mentioning refreshments would be served and invited them to bring their friends and relatives along. (People are more comfortable bringing someone they know with them to shop at a private house, so would be happy to do so). I suggested the best time and day would be a Sunday afternoon, from one to five PM, and they make some cookies and finger cakes to serve along with coffee, set up in the kitchen, where everyone could serve themselves.

Several weeks later on a Monday morning, I received a lovely call from her thanking me for my advice. She said it was the most profitable venture they had ever had, far above their expectations. Not only did they sell most of their huge inventory, but they were working very hard to fill all their orders before Christmas. She has kept in touch with me and they now have their annual Christmas gift party, as well as a "men only" one for Valentines day, and another for Mother's Day.

They now give parties in other people's homes, with the hostess receiving a gift of jewelry according to the sales and future parties booked. Fund Raisers for different women's organizations has become another part of their business. These two imaginative and creative friends have become very successful entrepreneurs. Not only do they love what they do and have fun doing it, but they work their schedule to meet their needs.

One of the most satisfying rewards of my teaching experience came unexpectedly while visiting the grand opening of a brand new shopping square of posh boutique shops. Upon wandering into an elegant jewelry establishment with many people browsing, I heard someone call my name. Looking around I spotted Bonnie, one of my former students, standing behind one of the counters. She excitedly motioned me over and introduced me as her teacher to the owner of the store. She introduced him to me, as a talented jeweler and goldsmith and pointed out many pieces of jewelry as his handmade originals. He told me he appreciated the excellent quality of Bonnie's work and her wonderful expression of design. Showing me around the store, she proudly walked me over to a glass showcase mounted on the wall containing an exquisite display of her precious and semi-precious bead necklaces and bracelets. They were all so beautiful it would be difficult to select the one you liked best. She explained she was the "in house" pearl and bead stringer and would be custom designing beads for customers. She said the pieces in the showcase belonged to her, but she had an arrangment that would be mutually profitable for her and the owner. I left the store thinking how enterprising Bonnie was and what a very smart businessman this shopkeeper was!

For those of you who say you can't sell anything, just make and give your creations as gifts for Christmas, Chanukah, birthdays, etc. Design for that particular person's taste and you will see what happens.

There are many other ways to make money with your new found hobby and they're easy to find when you read the periodicals and magazines mentioned in the "Sources" chapter.

I hope you have enjoyed what you have read and above all, have learned the joy of beading!

Epilogue

I have shared most of what I have learned about beading with you and for whatever reason you bought this book, I wish you success and thank you.

I hope the reader feels I have written just the book I was searching for years and years ago -- a clearly written, very professional and graphic description of the fine art of pearl and bead stringing, enabling one to learn quickly and easily.

A very special thanks to those very special people who were so helpful to me in this endeavor.

Happy beading!

Description of Beads Shown on Back Cover

Horizontal Beads from Top to Bottom

8MM	*Natural Turquoise*
8MM	*White Howlite (NOTE: White Howlite is often dyed colors to simulate more expensive stones)*
8MM	*Coral*
8MM	*Yellow Jade*
12MM	*Natural Rose Quartz*
10MM	*Cape Amethyst*
6MM	*Green Jade*
8MM	*Mother of Pearl*

Vertical Beads from Right to Left

8MM	*Natural Lapis Lazulli with Cultured Pearls and Gold Beads*
8MM	*Carnelian with Gold Beads*
8MM	*Black Onyx with Silver and Gold Beads*
10MM	*Yellow Jade with Gold Beads*
6MM	*Malachite with Gold Beads*
8MM	*Hematite with Cultured Pearls and Marquisite Rondels*
10MM	*Blue Lace Agate with Silver Beads*
8MM	*Sodalite with Gold Beads*
10MM	*Turquoise Dyed White Howlite with Silver Beads*
12MM	*Bloodstone with Gold Beads*
10MM	*White Lace Agate with Gold Beads*
10MM	*Black Onyx with Gold Beads*
10MM	*Picture Jasper with Gold Rondels*

Old Treasures Restrung - Clockwise - 1. An enchanting *Trifari* bird pin circa 1940 flies again as the centerpiece of a fresh water pearl necklace using pin converters. 2. Retired pink beads awake amidst dazzling crystal, gold and cloisonne. 3. A three strand turquoise *Trifari* necklace circa 1920 reappears as a two strand bracelet and forty inch endless necklace. 4. Jet beads handed down to a fourth generation have a new twist with silver and black onyx.

Side Interest - Top to Bottom - 1. *Carved jade disc with cloisonne, gold, twisted and round black onyx beads. 2. Twists of gold among tiger eye beads with a dragon clasp. 3. Black agate hand carved fish swims amid black onyx and shiny gold. 4. Rhodonite beads are tied with a leopard jasper bow. 5. Carved fancy jasper medallion between red jasper, fancy jasper and gold beads.*

A Medley of Carved Accent Beads - Clockwise - 1. *A red jasper flower with gold cap and red jasper beads. 2. Red jasper floppy side bow. 3. Red jasper collar beads with round ones. 4. Kissing picture jasper fishes and gold bubbles on matching round beads. 5. Carnelian flower sparked with gold strung on Bostwana agate beads.*

Pinning Beads - Clockwise - 1. *Three strands of lapis lazuli chips twisted on a three strand pin converter and attached to a mother of pearl and marcasite pin. 2. A small diamond pin clasps forty inches of cultured pearls for a long lean look. 3. Marcasite and mother of pearl earrings. 4. Ninety-six inches of sterling silver beads wound into three strands and clasped at the side with a large bow pin.*

"A Thousand Points of Light" - *A sparkling crystal lariat.*

Twisted Affairs - Top to Bottom - 1. *Four strands of coral strung through lantern shaped and round shiny gold beads. 2. Four strands of mother of pearl peppered with tiny green jade beads on a two strand clasp. 3. Three strands of turquoise pulled through gold beads. 4. Black onyx, serpentine, amethyst, and red venetian glass beads spiced with gold on a four strand filigree clasp. 5. Four thirty-four inch ropes doubled and overlapped to make a knot necklace clasped at the back with a ring shortener.*

Wrist and Ear Adornments - Left to Right - 1. *Fresh water pearls woven with hematite beads.* 2.
Black onyx and gold drop earrings. 3. *Dark amethyst with decorative gold spacer bars.* 4.
Graduated cultured pearls with diamond and plain spacer bars. 5. *Black onyx with diagonal stripes
of gold beads and two spacer bars.* 6. *Half drilled pearl bead earrings.* 7. *Black onyx woven with
gold stripes.*

Two and Three Strand Chokers - Clockwise - 1. Two strands of pure white coral with gold accents. 2. Two strands of dark amethyst with gold caps separated with shiny gold round beads. 3. Three strands of rose quartz with a removable cloisonne centerpiece.